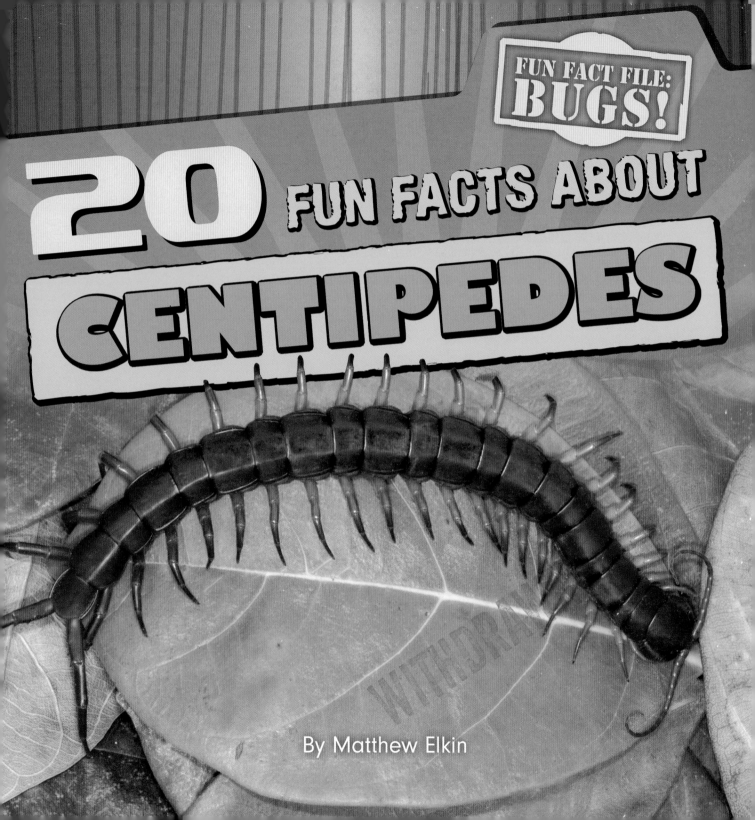

20 FUN FACTS ABOUT CENTIPEDES

By Matthew Elkin

Please visit our website, www.garethstevens.com. For a free color catalog of all our high-quality books, call toll free 1-800-542-2595 or fax 1-877-542-2596.

Library of Congress Cataloging-in-Publication Data

Elkin, Matthew.
 20 fun facts about centipedes / Matthew Elkin.
     p. cm. — (Fun fact file: bugs!)
 Includes index.
 ISBN 978-1-4339-8231-6 (pbk.)
 ISBN 978-1-4339-8232-3 (6-pack)
 ISBN 978-1-4339-8230-9 (library binding)
 1. Centipedes—Miscellanea—Juvenile literature. I. Title. II. Title: Twenty fun facts about centipedes.
 QL449.5.E55 2013
 595.6'2—dc23

                            2012021903

First Edition

Published in 2013 by
Gareth Stevens Publishing
111 East 14th Street, Suite 349
New York, NY 10003

Copyright © 2013 Gareth Stevens Publishing

Designer: Benjamin Gardner
Editor: Greg Roza

Photo credits: Cover, p. 1 jeridu/Shutterstock.com; p. 4 Pan Xunbin/Shutterstock.com; p. 5 © iStockphoto.com/Wong Hock Weng; pp. 6, 14 George Grall/National Geographic/Getty Images; p. 7 Awei/Shutterstock.com; p. 8 Audrey Snider-Bell/Shutterstock.com; p. 9 Pan Xunbin/Shutterstock.com; p. 10 (centipede) jefras/Shutterstock.com; p. 10 (lobster) Isantilli/Shutterstock.com; p. 11 © iStockphoto.com/jeridu; p. 12 John Mitchell/Oxford Scientific/Getty Images; p. 13 Photo Researchers/Getty Images; p. 15 Henrik Larsson/Shutterstock.com; p. 16 up close with nature/Flickr/Getty Images; pp. 17, 24 Dr. Morley Road/Shutterstock.com; p. 18 Scruggelgreen/Shutterstock.com; p. 19 Brooke Whatnall/Shutterstock.com; p. 20 © iStockphoto.com/Emmanouil Filippou; p. 21 Tom McHugh/Photo Researchers/Getty Images; p. 22 Suede Chen/Shutterstock.com; p. 23 Ryan M. Bolton/Shutterstock.com; p. 25 tomatito/Shutterstock.com; p. 26 Matthew Cole/Shutterstock.com; p. 29 © iStockphoto.com/Stephanie Asher.

Printed in the United States of America

CPSIA compliance information: Batch #CW13GS: For further information contact Gareth Stevens, New York, New York at 1-800-542-2595.

Contents

Words in the glossary appear in **bold** type the first time they are used in the text.

All Legs on Deck!

Centipedes are amazing creatures that are hard to find and often misunderstood. They're arthropods, which are animals that have a jointed **exoskeleton**, jointed legs, and no backbone.

Centipedes live all over the world. Most are nocturnal, which means they're active at night. This makes them hard to find during the day, when they often try to hide under leaves and rocks and in other dark, damp places. You might think centipedes are creepy, but they help keep your home free of other creepy creatures.

Some scientists think there may be about 8,000 species, or kinds, of centipedes in the world. So far, about 3,000 species have been recorded.

How Odd!

FACT 1

Centipedes can have many different numbers of legs.

With their long bodies, many legs, and fast, smooth movements, it's quite easy to recognize centipedes. Most people think that centipedes have 100 legs, but they usually don't. They can have fewer than 30 or more than 300 legs!

The word "centipede" comes from the Latin words for "hundred" and "foot."

6

house centipede

Centipedes always have an odd number of leg pairs.

Each **segment** of a centipede's body has two legs.

Centipedes always have an odd number of leg pairs.

Depending on the species, adult centipedes can have as few

as 15 leg pairs, like the house centipede, or as many as 191.

7

The centipede's venomous pinchers are sometimes called "poison claws."

FACT 3

Not all a centipede's legs are just legs.

Centipedes use their legs to run fast. However, the first pair below the centipede's head is a set of **venomous** pinchers. Centipedes use these legs like jaws to "bite" **predators** and catch **prey**. The last pair is a set of antennae, or feelers.

Centipede Anatomy

segments

antennae

legs

venomous
pincher

antennae

Centipede Bodies

FACT 4

Centipedes are more like lobsters and crabs than insects.

Although we call them bugs, centipedes aren't insects. They're arthropods, like lobsters and crabs. Arthropods have segmented bodies, a hard exoskeleton, jointed legs, and many pairs of limbs. Arthropod bodies have symmetry, which means they look the same on both sides.

lobster

Centipedes are a special type of arthropod called myriapods (MIHR-ee-uh-pahds). "Myriad" means "many," and "pod" means "foot."

house centipede

spiracles

Centipedes breathe through holes in their exoskeleton.

Centipedes don't breathe through their mouth. They breathe through holes in their exoskeleton called spiracles. Some species have spiracles on each segment, while others don't. Centipedes can't close their spiracles. This can cause them to lose a lot of moisture.

FACT 6

The biggest centipede is nearly 1 foot (30 cm) long.

Although centipedes can look a bit scary, most centipedes are tiny. The smallest centipedes are just a few millimeters long. However, the Amazonian giant centipede can grow to 12 inches (30 cm) long. That's bigger than an adult's hand!

The Life of a Centipede

Female centipedes can have over 60 babies at one time.

Female centipedes lay between 15 and 60 eggs, sometimes more, in soil or rotting wood. The eggs can take from 1 to several months to hatch. Once a baby centipede is born, it takes several years for it to become an adult.

A female centipede will protect her babies even after they have hatched.

FACT 8

Mother centipedes take good care of their eggs ... most of the time.

Female centipedes are known to stay close to their nests and keep their eggs safe. They lick the eggs to keep them clean. However, if something bothers the nest before the eggs hatch, the female may leave the eggs—or eat them!

Some centipedes eat their own mother once they hatch.

Some species of centipedes are matriphagic (ma-truh-FAY-jihk). This means the baby centipedes actually eat their mother soon

after they hatch! The babies use the **nutrients** from their mother's adult body to help them begin to grow.

This newly hatched centipede doesn't have a hard exoskeleton yet.

The blue-headed centipede, shown here, is common in Thailand. It's very fast and is known to bite.

FACT 10

Many centipedes add legs as they grow.

When centipedes are born, they may have no more than four pairs of legs. As they grow, they shed their skin, or molt, revealing a bigger body with new legs each time. Centipedes can go through as many as 10 molts in their lifetime.

Creepy Night Crawlers

Most centipedes will dry out and die in the sun.

We don't get to see centipedes very often. That's because they stay hidden most of the day. The sun's heat causes their bodies to lose water quickly. They prefer to hunt at night, when they're safe in the cool, moist air.

Centipedes often hide on the underside of leaves, where it's cool.

FACT 12

You might be living with centipedes.

Centipedes usually live outdoors in deep cracks and under rocks, but they also like damp areas inside your home. House-dwelling centipedes can lurk in dark cellars, bathrooms, and closets—and can live there for their entire life.

House centipedes, like this one, commonly live in homes to avoid the hot sun and cold winters.

Centipede Senses

Most centipedes have many eyes, but they can't see very well.

Although some centipedes have **compound eyes** like flies, most have groups of simple eyes on each side of their head. These eyes are called ocelli (oh-SEH-ly). They're not very strong, so most centipedes don't see well. Some centipedes don't have eyes at all!

Ocelli are good at identifying light and dark, but that's about it.

FACT 14

Since they can't see well, centipedes rely on other senses to help them stay alive.

Centipedes use their senses of touch and smell to move around and find prey. As nocturnal creatures, these senses help them to stay safe and well fed. Antennae at both ends of their body help them find their way around.

Carnivorous Creatures

Larger centipedes can catch snakes, birds, and bats.

Centipedes are carnivores. That means they eat only meat. They feed mostly on smaller arthropods. Some of the larger centipedes have been known to attack and feed on frogs, toads, small mammals, snakes, birds, and bats.

This large centipede has caught a rat.

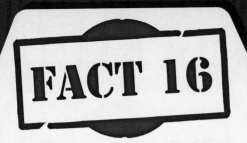

FACT 16

The centipede's venomous pinchers make them different from all other creatures in the animal kingdom.

The centipede's venomous legs are called forcipules (FOHR-suh-pyulz), and it's the only animal armed with them. Centipedes use their forcipules to **inject** a powerful venom into their prey. The larger the centipede, the stronger and more deadly the venom is.

Centipede venom can kill or stun prey, allowing the centipede to start eating.

Centipede venom can cause pain, swelling, and redness.

FACT 17

Centipedes can be dangerous to people who are allergic to bee stings.

Centipede bites can be painful, but they're usually not deadly. Their venom is much more dangerous for small animals. Centipede bites can feel like painful bee stings. People who are **allergic** to bee stings can also have bad reactions to centipede venom.

Centipedes for Dinner

Centipedes are eaten by mammals, insects, reptiles ... and people!

Even though they're swift hunters, centipedes are prey for many larger predators. These include birds, toads, rats, spiders, and other centipedes. In some parts of the world, people enjoying munching on centipedes, too! Many centipedes are stepped on by creatures that don't see them.

A spider enjoys a tasty lunch after a centipede wanders onto its web.

Centipedes have many ways to stay safe from enemies, including dropping off legs.

Some centipedes use **camouflage** to hide from predators. Others have bright colors that warn predators they're no good to eat. Many centipedes can drop off legs when predators grab onto them. This allows them to run away. The legs will grow back!

Centipede Cousins

FACT 20

Centipedes have cousins called millipedes.

Centipedes are sometimes confused with their many-legged relatives, millipedes. Unlike their carnivorous cousins, millipedes are slow-moving, plant-eating myriapods. They have two pairs of legs on most body segments instead of the single pair that centipedes have.

Centipedes and millipedes are often confused with one another, but they're very different.

Centipedes and Millipedes

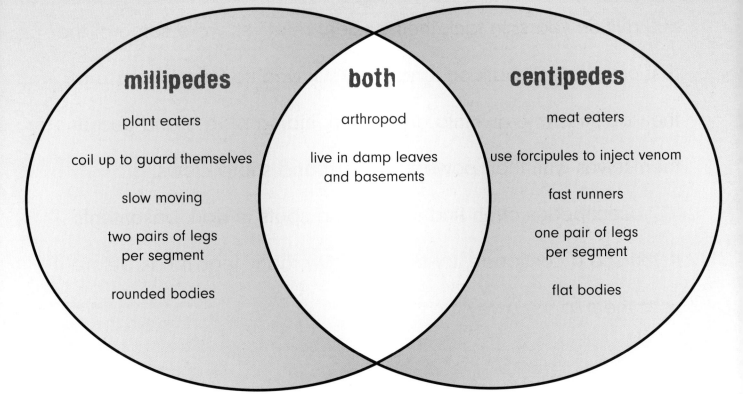

millipedes

plant eaters

coil up to guard themselves

slow moving

two pairs of legs
per segment

rounded bodies

both

arthropod

live in damp leaves
and basements

centipedes

meat eaters

use forcipules to inject venom

fast runners

one pair of legs
per segment

flat bodies

While they're both arthropods,
centipedes and millipedes have
several key differences.

Centipedes on the Run

Centipedes and other myriapods have been around for over 400 million years! In fact, their ancient relatives were some of the first creatures to walk on land. They've lived so long because of their abilities to crawl into deep, dark hiding places and guard themselves with their powerful venom and sharp claws.

Centipedes often find safe hiding spots in dark basements. If you see a centipede, try to count how many legs it has before it uses them to run away!

They may look creepy, but house centipedes eat other pests, such as cockroaches and silverfish.

Glossary

allergic: to be sensitive to normally harmless things in the surroundings, such as dust, pollen, or mold

camouflage: colors or shapes in animals that allow them to blend with their surroundings

compound eye: an eye made up of many separate seeing parts

exoskeleton: the hard outer covering of an animal's body

inject: to use sharp teeth or claws to force venom into an animal's body

nutrient: something a living thing needs to grow and stay alive

predator: an animal that hunts other animals for food

prey: an animal that is hunted by other animals for food

segment: a part of an insect's body

venomous: able to produce a liquid called venom that is harmful to other animals

For More Information

Books

Bonotaux, Gilles. *Dirty Rotten Bugs? Arthropods Unite to Tell Their Side of the Story.* Minnetonka, MN: Two-Can, 2007.

Rockwood, Leigh. *Centipedes and Millipedes Are Gross!* New York, NY: Powerkids Press, 2011.

Websites

House Centipedes
ento.psu.edu/extension/factsheets/house-centipedes
Read more about house centipedes.

Kentucky Centipedes
www.uky.edu/Ag/CritterFiles/casefile/relatives/centipedes/centipede.htm
Learn more about centipedes and see pictures of them.

Index